ZOOS
PAST & PRESENT

We humans are great collectors. We collect almost anything from old bottles to vintage cars. We also collect animals, keeping domesticated ones as pets or for farming, and "wild" species in zoos or wildlife parks.

In 1975 I joined the Auckland Zoo in New Zealand and spent nearly five years working there. It was at a time when many important changes were taking place, involving the image of zoos and what they stood for.

You may be one of the 330 million people who visited a zoo during the past year, but have you ever wondered how zoos started, why they exist, and what they might be like in the future? In this book you will find some answers to these questions, and I hope you will discover that zoos are far more than just places that display animals.

A Read-about

WRITTEN BY GRAHAM MEADOWS

These ancient cave paintings at Lascaux in France were drawn by people who had studied animals.

The dog was one of our earliest animal companions.

HOW DID ANIMAL COLLECTIONS START?

From evidence found by archaeologists we know that our ancestors collected, kept and studied animals many thousands of years ago.

Between thirty and sixty thousand years ago dogs were living in human camps in Europe, and there is a wealth of evidence to show that humans were interested in animals not just because they hunted them but also because certain animals could provide companionship.

Early man clearly wanted to study and learn more about animals, too. The famous cave paintings at Lascaux in France, which are at least 15,000 years old (perhaps very much older), were done by people who could be described as zoologists as well as artists.

The dog was almost certainly the first animal species to be domesticated by humans. Other species were also collected, and we know that by about 9,000 years ago many groups and tribes of people kept animals for use in hunting, as pets or for food. They included dogs, cats and different kinds of bird, including geese. The collection or domestication of birds and mammals continued throughout Europe and Asia.

Pigeons were probably domesticated in Iraq about 6,500 years ago.

The ancestors of our modern chicken were domesticated about 5,500 years ago in India.

3

About 5,000 years ago the Chinese and Egyptians kept collections of animals which contained undomesticated species such as giraffes and leopards, and other species that we associate with modern zoos.

Some Chinese princes owned deer parks and about 3,000 years ago Emperor Wen Wang established a zoological garden which he named Ling-Yu, or Garden of Intelligence, in which he kept exotic animals. Clearly he was concerned with learning as well as with pleasure.

By about 2,500 years ago the Greeks had developed a particular interest in birds, which included Egyptian geese, pigeons, chickens, ducks, and even talking parrots. They also commonly kept monkeys.

After the invasion of India the Greeks discovered the value of keeping elephants for work and for fighting battles. Alexander the Great kept Indian and African elephants, monkeys, bears and various other animals. Aristotle used them to study natural history. Shortly after Alexander's death in 321 BC the greatest zoo that the world had known was founded by King Ptolemy I at Alexandria.

(Above) The ancient Greeks kept African guinea-fowl and peacocks.

(Left) The Indian elephant was used in warfare about two thousand years ago.

(Below) Monkeys were favourites in early Greek zoos too.

Owning a lion or tiger made people feel tant.

e) New World animals such as the spider ey appeared in zoos after the discovery of nericas.

By the time Christ was born many wealthy Romans had established small private zoos in the grounds of their villas, but most nobles kept exotic animals merely to show off.

Many exotic animals were given away as gifts. About 900 years ago William the Conqueror built a country home in England and was given a bear as a housewarming present!

As time went by, not only rich people kept unusual animals. About 600 years ago there were travelling menageries in Europe. Animals such as bears were kept by animal trainers who taught them to perform simple tricks. Together they travelled from one town to another, following the fairs and entertaining the crowds.

Columbus explored the "new world" and found previously unknown animals. In South America the early explorer Cortés discovered a menagerie owned by Montezuma, which was so large that it needed a staff of 300 keepers!

The earliest explorers brought back dead animals, but soon live animals were being collected for scientific study and display in menageries. But almost all the early menageries were for the private enjoyment of their owners or selected visitors.

HOW DID ZOOS DEVELOP?

The public zoo as we know it evolved over three hundred and fifty years ago.

Louis XIV was one of the earliest zoo developers. He built the Menagerie du Parc at Versailles in 1624, where he not only kept animals but also planted greenery. This resulted in the name "zoological garden", rather than "menagerie", being given to such places.

More and more people became interested in animals and plants, and in 1824 a group of scientists formed a zoological society and built a zoological garden on a site at Regent's Park in London.

In 1828 it was opened to the British public who quickly developed a new slang name for it: "zoo." That name soon became applied to all such places.

These pictures show Regent's Park Zoo, London, in the early 19th Century, a few years after it was opened to the public.

Since then hundreds of zoos have been built throughout the world. About one fifth of them are in the United States.

In Australia, zoos were established at Melbourne in 1857, Adelaide in 1883, Perth in 1898 and Sydney in 1916.

Many of the early zoos were built and run by zoological societies but some city authorities also built zoos. Examples of these municipal zoos are the Wellington Zoo (1908) and the Auckland Zoo (between 1926 and 1931) in New Zealand.

Privately owned zoos were also established, such as Woburn in England and the Catskill Game Farm in America.

There are 550 zoos throughout the world. Thirty-four have been in existence for more than one hundred years.

About 330 million people visit zoos every year, and several zoos have annual attendances in excess of 5 million people.

Some zoos cover more than 500 hectares (1300 acres); others are less than 4 hectares (10 acres).

Some zoos, like those in London and San Diego, have very large animal collections with hundreds of different species. Others, like the Jersey Zoo in the Channel Islands, specialise in just a few types of animal.

(Opposite) The fringe-eared oryx and the white-bearded gnu live in the East African exhibit in the San Diego Wild Animal Park.

The San Diego Zoo, established in 1922, has a large collection of animals. (Above) The zoo's Cascade Canyon was laid out to take advantage of the natural features of the land.
(Below) The sun highlights a group of Chilean flamingos in another part of the Wild Animal Park.

(Above left) The jaguar, largest of the New World cats, is now becoming scarce in the wild.

(Above right) Only a few zoos outside China display red pandas.

(Below) The sea-lion is one of the most popular animals in the zoo, especially at feeding time.

WHAT IS A ZOO FOR?

To Display Animals

Zoos differ from places like museums or art galleries in one important respect. Whereas the latter display objects, zoos display living things.

One of the main purposes of a zoo is to display animals, particularly those species that the visitor cannot normally get to see elsewhere.

To Provide Enjoyment

A good zoo certainly aims to entertain its visitors, but these days entertainment doesn't mean chimpanzee tea parties or animal rides.

A more enlightened public can get just as much enjoyment from watching animals behaving naturally in natural surroundings, and from looking at some of the excellent educational displays and exhibits that most zoos now provide.

Of course feeding time at the zoo is as popular as ever.

12

(Above) A keeper shows a wombat to young visitors at the Children's Zoo at the Auckland Zoo.

(Below) A San Diego Zoo veterinarian examines an anaesthetised orang-utan, while its baby looks on.

To Educate

Modern zoos also try to educate their visitors in several ways. They have attractive signs and information boards that give people basic facts about the animals that they are watching. They publish comprehensive zoo guides. And many zoos also have teachers on their staff who take school and adult classes and show slides, films and videos.

To Study Animals

Many major zoos carry out scientific study and research that will benefit both zoo and wild animals. One example is artificial breeding, which can eliminate the need to catch more animals from the wild.

To Breed Animals

Another of a zoo's objectives is the breeding of animals.

In the early days zoos were consumers of wildlife, because most animals did not live very long in captivity and a large number died during capture or transit from the wild. For every orang-utan that ended up in a zoo, about twenty others died along the way. But even so, the losses from zoo trade were very small compared with those from the trade in animal skins and curios, a trade which continues even today.

These days most zoos try to be producers, not consumers, of wildlife by breeding all the replacements they need and providing a surplus for other zoos. There is international agreement to control zoo trade in wild animals.

Lessons learned from breeding common species like the giraffe and the puma can help zoos to breed endangered species like the gorilla.

To Contribute to Conservation

Successful breeding programmes can assist with the preservation and conservation of rare and endangered species. This subject is dealt with more fully in the companion book in this series: *Endangered Species.*

Those zoos that keep rare animal species also co-operate with other zoos in order to give the animals the best possible breeding conditions.

Individual animals are often lent or given from one zoo to another so that they can be found a suitable mate, and in some cases everyone has agreed that the animals should not belong to any one zoo but be regarded as an international asset.

I have written more about the way zoos can help to save rare animals in *Endangered Species.*

Visit your local zoo and find out if they are breeding any rare or endangered species.

(Top left), the California condor and the Arabian oryx (Above), the tiger (Below) and the polar bear (Right).

WHAT MAKES A ZOO?

A zoo is a bit like a jigsaw puzzle: it is made up of a number of different pieces.

Land and Location

Many of the older zoos were built close to towns or cities because in those days very few people owned cars. Most visitors walked, or caught a tram or bus.

Now most families own a car and can travel quite long distances, so modern zoos are often built in the country away from populated areas. The land there is less expensive, so the animals can have larger, more natural enclosures. Many of these country zoos are owned by city zoos. Examples are Whipsnade, associated with London Zoo, and the San Diego Wildlife Park, an extension of the San Diego Zoo.

16

(Above) Tall giraffes need a special house and plenty of space outside.

(Below) The zebra is another grazing animal which is suited to display in modern grassy enclosures.

Buildings and Enclosures

Most zoo animals are not tame and must be kept separate from visitors.

Their enclosure usually consists of two parts: an outdoor area where the animals can get plenty of exercise, and an indoor area where they can shelter from the sun or the rain, or be kept warm during the winter. Modern enclosures make the maximum use of natural materials and many have moats or glass-fronted areas to make viewing easier.

Why do you think cement floors are used in many of the older zoo enclosures?

17

(Top) This chimpanzee is enjoying the play structure provided in its enclosure.

(Below left) Antelopes have space for grazing in the ungulates' enclosure at the Auckland Zoo.

(Below) The aquarium at Taronga Park Zoo, Sydney, provides an underwater view of the swimming movements of sea-lions.

Special areas may also be needed to house animals that are sick or injured, or females with newly born young.

Some animals need specially designed enclosures. Fish are housed in an aquarium, and giraffes need special housing because of their height. Nocturnal animals need a special house with dim lighting so that they will be active during the day when the public wants to see them.

What other animals can you think of that need special enclosures?

Grounds and Gardens

Most zoos are true zoological gardens and have well-cared-for lawns, flower beds and shrubberies.

(Above) The felling of South American jungles has caused animals like this golden lion tamarin to become endangered species.

(Below) This heavily planted enclosure, with indoor and outdoor areas, provides an ideal environment for the jungle-dwelling tamarin.

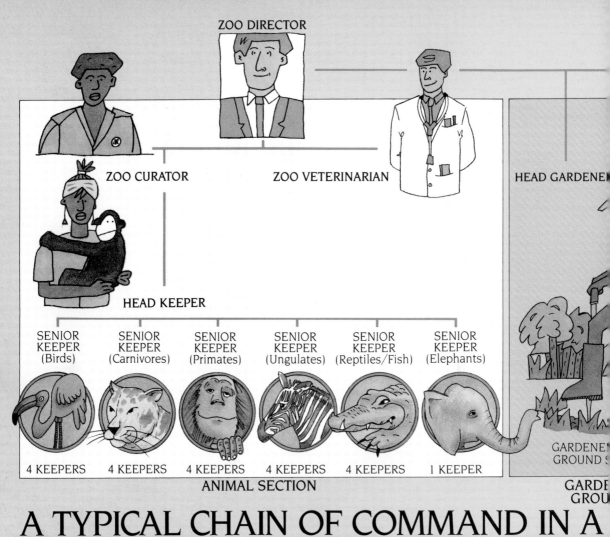

ZOO DIRECTOR

ZOO CURATOR

ZOO VETERINARIAN

HEAD GARDENER

HEAD KEEPER

SENIOR KEEPER (Birds)	SENIOR KEEPER (Carnivores)	SENIOR KEEPER (Primates)	SENIOR KEEPER (Ungulates)	SENIOR KEEPER (Reptiles/Fish)	SENIOR KEEPER (Elephants)
4 KEEPERS	4 KEEPERS	4 KEEPERS	4 KEEPERS	4 KEEPERS	1 KEEPER

ANIMAL SECTION

GARDENE
GROUND S

GARDE
GROU

A TYPICAL CHAIN OF COMMAND IN A

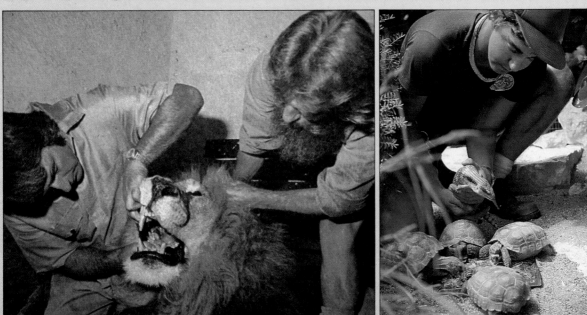

SECRETARY   MANAGER

GATE KEEPERS   RESTAURANT
CASHIERS   & CAFETERIA STAFF

ADMINISTRATION
& PUBLIC AMENITIES

L ZOO

(Left to right) The author looks at a lion's broken tooth while working as a zoo veterinarian.
A keeper feeds tortoises and a blue-tongued lizard in the reptile enclosure at Auckland Zoo.
A keeper hand-rears a jaguar cub whose mother cannot feed it.

People

A zoo could not function without the people who work there.

The **director** is in charge and must make sure that the zoo runs smoothly and pays its way.

The **curator** is responsible for the animal collection, and is often a trained zoologist. Large zoos may have several curators, each responsible for a different group of animals.

Keepers carry out the day-to-day care and feeding of the animals. There is usually a **head keeper** in charge of them.

Many zoos employ a **veterinarian** to ensure proper health and to treat sick or injured animals. I was veterinarian at the Auckland Zoo.

As I said earlier, education is one of a modern zoo's objectives. Many zoos employ one or more **teachers** who have their own classrooms or lecture halls.

Gardening staff, led by a **head gardener**, look after the zoo grounds. Other staff are employed to keep pathways and roads clean, and to carry out day-to-day repairs. People are needed to serve snacks and meals, sell souvenirs and collect money at the gate!

Zoos also employ specialists from time to time, such as architects to design new buildings and enclosures.

Animals

Without animals a zoo wouldn't exist. Many of the early zoos tried to display as many animals as possible, including unusual species, in order to attract visitors. These days most zoos limit the size of their collections and are concerned about protecting wildlife.

In the old days zoos often used to display animals in no particular order, but now many arrange for species from a particular region of the world to be shown together or next to each other. This is called a zoogeographic exhibit. Common areas of the world used for zoogeographic exhibits are North America, South America, Eurasia, Africa and Australasia.

Some zoos develop displays that reflect a particular theme, such as "World of Birds", "The Tropical Rainforest", or "The Living Desert".

Almost every zoo has a section known as the Children's Zoo, where tame animals can be seen at close quarters or even touched. These are both fun and educational. For example, the Children's Zoo at the Bronx Zoo was planned so that children could explore five major areas: how and where animals live, their methods of locomotion, their means of defence, their senses, and their association with man.

Carry out a survey among your school class to find out which animal species are the most popular or unpopular.

The survival of all these animals could depend on zoos.
(Above) The tuatara is now found only on a few offshore islands of New Zealand.
(Below left) The Przewalski horse became extinct in the wild, but the species was saved because some animals had been kept in zoos.
(Below right) Rhinoceros are hunted for their horns, and will probably become extinct, except in reserve areas and zoos.

22

ARE ZOOS NECESSARY?

Some people think that zoos are cruel places that are no longer necessary. They argue that we can learn more about animals by watching wildlife films.

Modern, reputable zoos are not cruel places. I have visited almost fifty of the world's major zoos and I know that they give their animals the best possible care and attention, which is often better than many people give their own pet animals.

Some of their animals have been bred and born in captivity for generations and are well adapted to life in comfortable zoo surroundings. Indeed, many of them are so used to being fed and looked after that if they were released into the wild they would probably not survive.

Zoos should not take further animals from the wild unless it is to save their lives or their species from extinction.

Of course we can, and should, learn as much as possible from films and television, but the zoo offers us a unique opportunity to actually see and smell a particular living creature.

Remember also that when a species becomes highly endangered in the wild its survival can depend on the captive breeding of those individuals held in zoos.

WHAT IS THE FUTURE OF ZOOS?

The zoo of the future will continue the work done by today's zoos. It will aim never to take animals from the wild except in the cause of conservation, and it will promote the cause of conservation to the public.

It will concentrate on the care and breeding of selected species. It will develop even better enclosures for its animals, and viewing areas for the public. It will develop education programmes for people of all ages and make more use of computers and modern sound systems.

Where suitable it will conduct scientific research that will benefit animals but do them no harm, such as the deep freezing of eggs and embryos to preserve genetic material for the future.

Whatever the zoo of the future may be, a zoo should be judged not on whether it keeps rare or unusual species, but by the way in which it houses, cares for and displays its animals.

(Top) A mock termite mound in this ape enclosure allows the animals to behave naturally and enables scientists to study their "tool"-using behaviour.

(Above) Feeding time gives an opportunity for zoo staff to teach people about the animals.